Enron: Crooks In Suits

The Story of Enron and the Biggest Corporate Scandal In History

Phil Coleman

Copyright © 2017.

All rights reserved. No part of this publication may be reproduced, distributed, or transmitted in any form or by any means, including photocopying, recording, or other electronic or mechanical methods, without the prior written permission of the publisher, except in the case of brief quotations embodied in critical reviews and certain other noncommercial uses permitted by copyright law.

This book is intended for informational and entertainment purposes only. The publisher limits all liability arising from this work to the fullest extent of the law.

Table of Contents

Introduction

ENRON – The Beginning

JEDI, CHEWCO, WHITEWING, LJM, RAPTORS ……Where will it stop?

What Enron Did With Lobbyist!

Enron's Auditors & Auditing

I Think This Will Be Our Easiest Year Yet……

January 13th, 2002 – It Was Not Going to be a Good Year

The Two Dirtiest Dogs In The Fight …

Those Who Suffered – It Was Not Right

Conclusion

Introduction

When you hear the word "Enron," the word scandal pops into your mind automatically. It was big, it was awful, it was ugly. It brought out a lot of change in all corporate America, even down to the industry to where I worked. We are trained on it every year. We must learn Sarbanes-Oxley, like it is a Bible Verse, so something like this never happens again.

I do not think at the inception of this company that it was ever intended to go this direction. I believe that some of the leaders got increasingly greedy and smug and greedier and there was just not enough money to satisfy all the greed they had in their hearts.

I feel confident if you told them that money does not buy you happiness, they would disagree and say, but you sure can have fun with it.

One or two things may happen in a company that might show up on the books that do not look good. But, with Enron, there was so much effort put into covering up so many issues that it took someone much brighter than me to know how to "cook the books" so to speak and make it happen.

They kept it up for quite some time too.

Did they do this deliberately? At the inception, do you think they started out to defraud everyone? Read right on my friend and decide for yourself. You will get to be the judge by the end of the book.

ENRON – The Beginning

Enron was initially formed by Ken Lay in 1985. But not before it had merged with InterNorth and Houston Natural Gas.

Ken Lay; born in Texas County, Missouri in the little town of Tyrone. He was from very modest beginnings as he one of the three children of his mother and father who was a struggling preacher and business man.

He moved to Columbia, Missouri and attended the University of Missouri and that is where he studied economics. In 1964, he graduated with a B.A. in then in 1965 an M.A. In 1970; he earned his Ph.D. in economics at the University of Houston. When he left there, he went to work for

Exxon Company. He started out working as a federal energy regulator.

Lay was friends with the Bush family, and this included the then Vice President George H.W. Bush. Lay made substantial monetary contributions, he led committees for the Republican Party and was even the co-chair for Bush's 1992 re-election.

Don't get it wrong; Ken Lay was dug dip into the Clinton Administration as well. Enron gave the Democrats $1.5 million in what they called soft and hard money contributions. Enron had gained 'privileged' access to the administration of the Clintons as well.

Enron, as a matter of fact, was one of Clinton's economic diplomacy primary beneficiaries, which promoted interests of the U.S. businesses abroad. Most of the money received by Enron from Exlm Bank and OPIC had been granted to them during the years of the Clinton Administration.

But, Enron was deeply dug into the Bush Family long before any of the presidential campaigns had ever started. Since Enron was a Houston-based trading company of the utility type that is set up to sell energy to its consumers; and its standing owes no small part to the fact of the Bush's governorship in the great state of Texas.

Texas in 1992 passed an Energy Policy Act that opened a black hole that allowed Enron to thrive and forced utility companies to have to buy their energy from Enron. Meanwhile, in our nation's capital, at the Commodity Futures Trading, under George

Herbert Walker Bush, they allowed for an exemption for trading energy subsidiaries. But, this practice would later come to be Enron's downfall.

The 1992 trading commission happened to be chaired by one, Wendy Gramm, who was the wife of Senator Phil Gramm of Texas and a close friend of the Bushes and had also received $97,350 of donations for politics from Enron. Enron was so congenial that they helped everyone in politics.

Once they got the exemption through, one Wendy Gramm, left as chair of the commission and joined the Enron board. She, as a matter of fact, was on the audit committee.

To muddy the waters a bit more. Enron wanted to get into Pennsylvania which was one of the biggest energy consumers in America. But, Enron was having trouble getting into Pennsylvania. So, Ken Lay called up Bush. George W. called up Tom Ridge and gave him a sales pitch on Enron and telling him how good that Enron was and what a serious company they were. Boom! Enron was in the energy market in Pennsylvania. Boom, Tom Ridge, governor of Pennsylvania promoted to Secretary of Homeland Security. See how easy that was?

Oh, but it didn't stop there! Carl Rove held $250,000 in Enron Stock, Defense Secretary, Donald Rumsfeld, Mark Weinberger, Kathleen Cooper, Eugene Hickock, ambassadors to Russia, Ireland, and officials that worked in the energy department.

Enron was so tight with the Bush Administration that Ken Lay and other Enron Execs got called to the White House for six different meetings with Dick Cheney and his staff.

As President, Lay would fly Bush and his wife Barbara to Washington on Enron's corporate plane. As a matter of fact, in December 2000, Lay had been mentioned to be a possible candidate for Treasury secretary.

From 1989 – 2002 Lay's contributions to 'politics' was $5.8 million. It was said that 73% went to the Republicans and that 27% went to the Democrats.

In the year 1999, Lay was one if not the highest paid CEOs in the United States with a compensation package of $42.4 million.

From 1998 to 2001, in stock options alone, Lay liquidated more than $300 million from Enron.

It was the first natural gas pipeline network that went nationwide.

Ken Lay did not stop there; in the early 1990s, he aided in starting up the sale of electric at market prices. Not long after that move, the U.S. Congress approved legislation that would 'deregulate' the sale of natural gas.

Due to this, Enron was selling energy for big money due to its higher prices. Interesting to note that George Herbert Walker Bush was President of the United States at that time.

The same George Herbert Walker Bush whose name had been tied to the JFK assassination as well as the Nixon Watergate fiasco. Anytime there is something dirty that is taking place; his name always pops up in the middle of it all, in case you had not noticed.

And, we find out that he and Ken Lay are good friends along with Dick Cheney, who would be the future Vice President of the United States with the younger Bush. Quite strange bedfellows I would say, but when it comes to oil and money; I guess the two must mix somehow.

It allowed traders like Enron to be able to sell their energy at higher prices.

And you can bet that they did. Enron ran schemes they used to defraud different officials that were running California's power grid. They were manipulating the energy supplies and thoroughly looting California's treasury of billions. During this period, Enron was very tight with the Bush White House. They had made sure that appeals from California officials asking for federal intervention to impose price caps on the energy supplies were rejected.

People living in California had to suffer through six full days of blackouts early in the year 2001 which followed a tenfold increase in their energy prices. The price hikes alone brought on near collapse and bankruptcy of two large utility companies. Thousands of workers were laid off.

State officials had to impose severe cuts to the budget because of the extreme rise in energy costs that had risen from $7 billion to $27 billion within 12 months.

Sickeningly one of Enron's strategies involved buying electricity from the state of California Power Exchange and paying $250 per megawatt/hour which was the max allowed by state law. Then they would resell it to other states in the North Pacific for $1,200.

It contributed to more shortages in California. Enron flooded California's transmission lines with so much electricity that it couldn't handle it causing "congestion payments" to be collected from Cal-ISO.

They said that because of the congestions charges being so high, it might be profitable to sell the power at a loss just to collect the congestion payment.

Investigators would later find they were "megawatt laundering," by which Enron would buy power in California – at low capped cost – then resell it out of state and then bring it back to resell it to California with a huge markup. Therefore, Enron, by selling to California "out of state" Electric, Enron could get around the price restrictions on the power that had been bought in California.

When Ken Lay was interviewed on PBS about this, he said, "Every time there's a shortage or a little bit of a price spike, it's always collusion or conspiracy or something. I mean, it always makes people feel better that way."

Bush administration folks said that California's problems were caused by the states own "flawed" plan on deregulation plan and their environmental standards that were so strict therefore limiting them on building new power plants. Both Cheney and Bush publicly opposed any price controls.

Oil producers and the local governments were having a fit and rightly so with all the price unpredictability, and they started asking for regulation. There was some intense lobbying taking place on Enron's part, and it put a stop to the law.

It all put together made Enron the biggest dealer/seller in North America of natural gas by 1992. Just its gas trading contracts were earning $122 million (and that was prior to interest and taxes), and they were the second largest donor toward the company's net income.

By November 1999 EnronOnline had been created for their trading website, and it allowed them to better oversee its contracts in the trading business.

Enron decided that if they were going to grow that they needed to diversify. Since they already owned and operated several assets that included electricity plants, paper and pulp plants, gas pipelines, broadband services around the globe, and water plants; it was decided to gain more revenue by getting more of the same products with which they were already involved.

It would mean building power generation plants in underdeveloped countries like The

Philippines (in Subic Bay), India (Dabhol), and Indonesia.

With Enron's natural gas side of business, the accounting team had been easy, and straightforward.

For each quarter, the company would list actual costs associated with supplying the gas and the actual revenues from selling the gas. But, when Skilling came on board, he did not want it done this way, he said that they would handle it by adopting mark-to-market accounting.

Skilling said that it would show 'true economic value.' Thus, Enron was the first non-financial group to use this method to report its hard to understand long-term contracts.

When you utilize the Mark-to-market accounting, it requires that once the contract gets signed, the income is to be estimated at the present value of net future cash flow. What was bad, often, the durability of these contracts and their costs were hard to predict.

Because of the enormous discrepancies of trying to match profits and cash, investors were usually given reports that were misleading or false. By using this method, income on these projects could go ahead and be recorded, even though there had not been once cent of money received. But, still making it look on the books like the earnings were increasing.

They would see in future years, that profits would not be allowed to include, so any additional or new income had to come from other projects to show/develop further growth that made the investors happy.

What did not make any sense; despite all the problems it could cause, the U.S. Securities and Exchange approved this accounting method so Enron could continue in its trading of natural gas futures.

Enron went on to expand this process to other areas in their company so they would meet Wall Street projections.

As an example: July 2000, Blockbuster Video and Enron signed a 20-year agreement. They would introduce on-demand videos to various U.S. cities by the end of the year.

After they had tested several pilots, Enron realized there could be profits of more than

$110 million with this deal. Analysts were shaking their heads about the technical viability and whether there would even be a market demand for this service. When it failed, Blockbuster withdrew. Enron however, continued to show future profits, even when the deal resulted in a loss.

Enron then used what they called 'special purpose entities' which were nothing more than limited partnerships that they created to fill a specific or temporary purpose to manage or fund risks that were associated with 'specific' assets.

The company made sure only to allow minimal details on how it used the 'special purpose entities.' They were merely shell companies that were created by some sponsor but got funded by different debt financing and independent equity investors.

Now, for the financial reporting purposes, there are a series of rules that dictate if a special purpose entity is separate from the sponsor.

In 2001, all totaled, Enron was using hundreds of the special purpose entities for hiding its debts. They used partnerships like the Thomas and Condor for tax shelters, (FASITs) financial asset securitization investment trusts in what was called the Apache deal, they used (REMICs) in the Steele contract, real estate mortgage investment conduits, and then REMICs and (REITs) in the Cochise deal.

The special purpose entities were being used for far more than just getting around the general accounting conventions. Because of just one violation, Enron's balance sheet was a mess. It understated its liabilities and then overstated its equity, and then its earnings were overstated.

Enron thought they would be smart and told their shareholders that they were hedging downside risk by using the special purpose entities in its liquid investments.

The investors had no idea whatsoever that these special purpose entities were doing nothing but taking Enron's very own financial guarantees and its stock to finance these hedges.

It kept Enron from the protection of the downside risk. Some of the names of the 'special purpose entities they came up with were: LJM, Whitewing, Chewco, and JEDI.

JEDI, CHEWCO, WHITEWING, LJM, RAPTORS ......Where will it stop?

During 1993, Enron worked on a joint venture on energy investments with a group called CalPERS, also known as the California state pension fund, and called the (JEDI) Joint Energy Development Investments.

Then comes 1997, and Skilling, who is now serving as the COO, has asked CalPERS to join Enron in what he called a separate investment.

Let's take a quick look at this new COO. There is not much to tell about Jeffrey

Skilling. He was born in Pittsburgh, Pennsylvania and got his MBA from Harvard. In 1990 Ken Lay hired him on at Enron. By 1997 he was the president and COO.

CalPERS wanted to do this, but it did not want any part of JEDI. Well, Enron didn't want to be showing any debt by assuming CalPERS' stake with JEDI on the balance sheets. So, CFO, Fastow decided there would be another special purpose entity they would bless with the name 'Chewco Investments Limited Partnership.'

As you see we have a new boy on the block; Andrew Fastow, the new CFO. He was born in Washington, D.C. He was one out of three sons raised in your regular middle-class Jewish family. They lived in Providence,

New Jersey. After he had earned his MBA from Northwestern U., he went to work for Continental Illinois National Bank and Trust Company in Chicago.

It helped raise the debt that was guaranteed by Enron, and they used it to purchase CalPER's joint venture for $383 million. Because Fastow created Chewco, JEDI's losses never saw the light of day on Enron's balance sheets.

Now, by the autumn of 2001, Enron's and CalPERS arrangement had been found out. It stopped Enron's prior accounting methodology for JEDI and Chewco. Since this was revealed, it showed that Enron's earnings from 1997 to mid-2001 should be reduced by $405 million and then the company would further slide into indebtedness of $628 million.

Along comes Whitewing in December 1997 as a 'special purpose entity' also being used as another financing method by Enron. It was funded by $579 million being provided by Enron and another $500 million by some 'outside' investor. They called themselves, Whitewing Associates, L.P. In a couple of years, the arrangement of the entity was changed so that it would not be connected with Enron and would not be counted then on the company's balance sheets.

They used Whitewing to purchase Enron assets, this included pipelines, stocks, other investments, and power plants. Between 1999 -2001, Whitewing bought out assets thru Enron worth $2 billion and they were using Enron stock as collateral.

Wow, what could be wrong with this? The transactions were being approved by the Board of Enron, and it must be above board. The asset transfers, however, were not real sales and never should have been treated as such but should have been treated as loans.

So, in 1999, Fastow made up two more limited partnerships: He gave them some long names, but it boiled down to LJM1 and LJM2, and they were made up for the sole purpose of getting rid of Enron's bad performing stocks and stakes to make its financial statements look better.

To be able to do this, Fastow had to go before the board of directors (who had no clue what was going on) to get an 'exemption' from Enron's Code of Ethics. Would that right there not make you sit up and take notice that something was not, quite right?

And, the board gave him their blessing apparently because the two partnerships of LJM1 and LJM2 wound up being funded with around $390 million that was given to them by who else but Merrill Lynch, Citigroup, Credit Suisse First Boston, J.P. Morgan Chase, Wachovia, and other investors as well.

At this point we see Enron transferring to "Raptor I-IV," four LJM-related special purpose entities now with more than "$1.2 billion in assets. That included shares in the millions of Enron common stock and on top of that long-term rights to buy millions of shares, along with $150 million just in Enron notes that were payable" as was disclosed in the company's financial statements. The "entities" had been used as a way to pay for all of this using the 'entities" debt instruments.

Because Enron jumped on the bandwagon and capitalized with the Raptors; they did so in such a way similar to accounting that is employed when a company goes out and will issue stock in a public offering. Then they booked the notes considered payable issued as assets on its balance sheets while they increased the shareholder's equity for the very same amount. It hurt them on down the line and became an issue for Enron and its auditor, Arthur Andersen because taking it off the balance sheet caused a $1.2

billion decrease in the shareholder's equity net.

It would eventually see the plagiarized contracts that were worth $2.1 billion losing significant value. They were careful to establish swaps when the stock price had achieved its maximum.

The next year, the portfolio value under those same swaps were found to fall $1.1 billion when the share prices went down. What this meant was that the 'special purpose entities' that they had set up now were owing Enron $1.1 billion per the contracts. Since Enron was using the "mark-to-market" accounting plan, it claimed a $500,000 million gain on those swap contracts on the face of its 2000 annual report.

This gain allowed for offsetting its stock losses and could show nearly a third of the earnings of Enron for 2000 (before 2001 when it was then correctly restated.)

If you just looked on paper, Enron had the 'model' board of directors. The one every corporation dreamed they could have. It was comprised of outsiders that had a very significant stake, and it also had a talented audit committee.

In the review of corporate boards in 2000, Chief Executive Magazine named Enron to be in the top five of best boards. Even though it had a complex governance and its network of intermediaries were also complex; Enron still had the ability to roll in massive sums of money, capital to fund very questionable business models. They could conceal what it was doing through a complex series of financing and accounting maneuvers, and then hype up its stock to levels that only one could dream.

Even though Enron's performance and compensation management system had been designed to keep and retain their most valuable employees, it was such a dysfunctional corporate culture. They all became so obsessed with the short-term just to get the biggest bonuses.

The employees were constantly trying to start deals, often without regard to the quality of profits or the cash flow, just to get a high rating in their performance review.

On top of that, they made sure that results from accounting were recorded as soon as they happened so they could keep up with Enron's stock price. By using this practice, it helped to ensure deal-makers and the executives still received their large cash bonuses as well as stock options.

To the public, Enron was always emphasizing how great its stock prices were doing. Management kept being compensated by using stock options, just like other U.S. companies.

The policy of awards by stock option was causing management to develop expectations of rapid growth to make it look like the reported earnings were meeting Wall Street's expectations. You would find the stock ticker everywhere; displayed on company computers, in the elevators, and in lobbies.

During budget meetings, Skilling himself would make up target earnings just by asking "what kind of profits do we need to see to keep our stock price up?" Skilling would use that number even if it was impossible and made no sense.

December 31, 2000, Enron had out 96 million shares that were outstanding as stock option plans. Enron's 'proxy' statement said that, in the next three years, these were going to be exercised. So, by using Enron's January 2001 $83.13 stock price along with the directors' ownership reported in the proxy for 2001, the predicted value of director stock was $659 million for just Lay and $174 million just for Skilling.

It was Skilling's belief that if their employees were worried about cost, that it could hinder original thinking. So, as a result, extravagant spending went crazy through the entire company, more so among the executives.

Now, the employees had lots of money at their disposal for their expense accounts and the executives were being paid twice as much as their competitors. For instance, in 1998, their top 200 employees who were the highest-paid received $193 million from their stock, bonuses, and salaries. Then in two years, that figure jumped up to $1.4 billion!

Before the scandal broke for the whole world to see, Enron was applauded for its savvy financial risk managing tools. Risk Management was extremely crucial for Enron not just because of its business plan, but its regulatory environment was risk-ridden at best.

Enron had been careful to establish fixed commitments for the long term that needed to be hedged for preparing ahead of the invariable future energy price fluctuations that would more than likely be seen.

Enron's bankruptcy downfall was because of its crazy use of special purpose entities and derivatives. It never made any sense. By the way, they hedged its risks with their 'special purpose entities' that it owned itself.

It caused Enron to retain the risks that were associated with all the transactions. By using this arrangement, it had Enron using hedges with itself!

Enron never hid any of this from the board of directors, as the Senate subcommittee did learn. And Enron's board was told about all the Raptor, LJM, and Whitewing, and then when they approved them got updates on their operations. Unfortunately, Enron's Board or Finance Committee didn't know enough to understand what was actually happening.

The Senate subcommittee felt that if the board had realized what was going on, they would have never let it happen.

What Enron Did With Lobbyist!

It blows one's mind what Enron did with all the lobbyists on their payroll. They were wining and dining everyone in Washington, D.C. to get what they wanted and get, they did.

For a few examples:

- George Herbert Walker Bush himself signed off on the Natural Gas Decontrol Act during 1989. It removed some regulatory problems that Enron was running into, and it included natural gas price control that had been mandated back in 1978. It eliminated price control for natural gas.

- Then, the FERC approved of the Mojave pipeline project, which was a partnership between El Paso Natural Gas and Enron. It was finally passed in 1990.
- Federal Energy Regulatory Commission decided to restructure the interstate pipeline operations in 1992. It separated out the transportation and the sales of the services. It would let the customer choose who they would get transportation services from and who they would choose to supply them with natural gas.
- There was a Tax credit to produce non-conventional fuels, under Section 29 of the IRS code, it was established somewhere in the Windfall Profit Tax Act. This meant that any wells dug in

1992 were eligible for the subsidy until about 2002. It was then extended multiple times in Congress thanks to good old Enron lobbying.
- The Securities and Exchange Commission exempted Enron from the PUHCA – Public Utility Holding Company Act, that banned utilities from being able to invest in potentially risky, and unrelated, business in 1993.
- In April 1996, the FERC set forth a couple of rules that were favorable to who else but Enron. The open-access rule that forced utility companies to unbundle transmission services and generation and bring in wholesale transmission transactions to an open-access transmitting tariff. The commission went on to order to help

states in the restructuring of the electric industry to allow retail consumers to be able to choose service providers.

- In 1997, the FERC Enron's merger with Portland General Corp. was approved by the FERC in record time. Per Enron, the first merger the FERC had approved since October 1994.
- In 1997, the Securities and Exchange Commission exempted Enron from the stipulations of the Investment Co. Act going back to 1940 that disallowed U.S. companies to leave debt from overseas projects off their books.
- 1998, Brooksley Born, Chief of the Commodity Futures Trading Commission, made a proposal to regulate the derivatives that had been

prompted by hectic lobbying used by Enron and other underwriters and derivative users. The proposal was opposed by Alan Greenspan and Robert Rubin, did not pass. As a matter of fact, Congress decided to pass a moratorium on derivative regulations.

- Enron and others wanted the 'alternative minimum tax to be repealed. What actually happened, however, was that the 1997 balanced-budget 'relaxed' the rules, thereby reducing tax liability for companies that buy new machinery.
- Enron was lobbying again. This time for what they called the NAFTA highway also known as the I-69 highway. It would bring the Canada

to Indiana highway down through Texas and into Mexico. Congress approved it in 1997.

- The tax credit for wind energy production – Enron was one of the biggest benefactors of that too! It was created in 1992, and extended every couple of years since.
- 1988 a bill from the Defense Dept. so they could purchase power from their local utility companies. After Enron's lobbying, the Pentagon decided to privatize the base services. In 1999, Enron grabbed a 10-year deal at the cost of $25 million to be the energy supplier for Fort Hamilton in New York.

- The African Growth Act. It was signed by Bill Clinton in 2000. It set the conditions for new aid and the trading benefits to the African states. One of the conditions was to open their economies to foreign trade.
- 2000, Congress approved increasing the amount of time that workers from other countries could come to the U.S. to work. It raised the limit of people from 115,000 to 195,000. Lay himself lobbied for this in Congress.
- FERC Order 367. In 2000, this order deregulated even more natural gas distribution by making the pipeline regulations stricter. One of the effects this had was the developing a market for natural gas commodity trading.

- Commodity Futures Modernization Act of 2000. It made it permanent that Enron could not be regulated on trading in energy derivatives.

That was only the bills that Enron wanted to be passed. There were nineteen bills that they wanted deregulation in different states and they did it. Enron made it happen.

Enron did not stop there; then they started lobbying for international issues. They just kept eating up everything they could get their hands on that would benefit them and their pocket books.

Enron's Auditors & Auditing

Enron had its corporate audit committees. Most usually they just met a few times each year. Their members usually did not have much experience with finance and accounting. Enron however, was different, their audit committee had expertise, they were no dummies.

Their audit committee included:

- Robert Jaedicke – accounting professor from Stanford University
- Paulo Pereira – prior CEO and president of State Bank in Brazil
- John Medelsohn – President, M.D. Anderson Cancer Center

- Ronnie Chan – businessman from Hong Kong
- John Wakeham – Secretary of State for Energy – prior from the United Kingdom
- Wendy Gramm – prior Commodity Futures Trading Commission Chair

Enron was accused that because its meetings were so brief that there was no way they could cover significant amounts of information. In February 2001, the audit committee met for 1½ hours. They didn't have enough knowledge to know what questions to ask the auditors on any of the accounting issues. They were unable to put questions to the management team because of pressures on the committee.

When they finally were investigated, the board was accused of letting conflicts of interest interfere with what their duties truly were in monitoring Enron's accounting practices.

Enron had a habit of 'cooking the books' or rather booking costs when they canceled projects they would claim them as assets. They used the rationale that there was no official letter to prove the project had been canceled. It was called the "snowball," and initially they were supposed to only use it on projects that were worth less than $90 million, they later increased it to $200 million.

When analysts would be taken on a tour of the Enron offices, everyone was always impressed with how hard the employees would be working. What was actually happening? Skilling would move other employees to that office (telling them to work hard) so as to create the look that they were bigger than they really were. They used this ploy many times over to fool analysts to help improve stock prices.

Enron had their own auditing firm, Arthur Anderson, and they were accused of shabby standards by the way they audited and conflict of interest because of huge consulting fees paid by Enron.

In 2000, Arthur Anderson racked up $25 million in just audit fees. In consulting fees, $27 million. This amount alone made up for about 27% of audit fees of all the public clients for Anderson's Houston office).

It could not be decided when the auditor's methods were questioned if they overlooked things on purpose because of how much money they were making off Enron or because they just did not know what they were doing and how to properly review Enron with the way accounting practices were set up.

Enron would hire numerous CPA's and accountants who had even worked on developing new accounting rules with the (FASB), Financial Accounting Standards Board. The new controllers searched for all kind of ways to try and save Enron money. That included trying to capitalize on loopholes that they found in (GAAP) Generally Accepted Accounting Principles, some of the standards used by the accounting industry.

One Enron accountant stated that they tried hard to use the (GAAP) to Enron's advantage. The rules created a lot of opportunities. We only got where we did by using that weakness.

Andersen's auditors, however, were pressured to look the other way by Enron to recognizing charges from "special purpose entities" as the credit risks were becoming known. Besides, the entities would not ever make a profit; the accounting guidelines made Enron take a write-off, then the value of the object was taken off the balance sheet, and it was done so at a loss.

To try and pressure Andersen to meet Enron's earnings expectations, Enron would occasionally allow other accounting companies like Ernst & Young or

PricewaterhouseCoopers to come in and complete some accounting tasks to make it look like they were hiring a new firm to replace Andersen.

Andersen itself, was well equipped with the internal controls to make sure to protect against incentives that may be conflicted of their local partners; but it failed in its ability to prevent conflict of interest.

There was one case, where Andersen's office in Houston that performed Enron's audit was successful in overruling critical reviews of Enron's decisions in accounting that had been given by Andersen's Chicago partner.

Then when news of the U.S. Securities and Exchange Commission (SEC) were investigating Enron became public, Anderson would shred tons (several) of documents that were relevant and then delete 30,000 computer files and emails, thereby causing the accusations of a cover-up.

The revelations about Andersen's performance overall caused the firm to break-up.

I Think This Will Be Our Easiest Year Yet……

And how famous those last words came to be.

Those words were uttered by Rick Causey as he told the budget managers. In his own words, he said: "From an accounting standpoint, this will be our easiest year ever. We've got 2001 in the bag."

Richard was pretty new to Enron. In 2001, he was the Chief Accounting Officer and Executive Vice President.

Before he came to Enron, he had been with Arthur Andersen & Co. in Houston where was a specialist in natural gas.

He had a Bachelor's Degree in business, and an accounting degree from U of T. He was a CPA.

In March of that year, Fortune magazine ran an article and had the question as a headline: Is Enron Overpriced? In the article, it goes on to ask how in the world Enron could keep its stock value so high for so long. It argues that all the investors and analysts could not figure out how Enron kept making its money.

The female journalist that first got involved with what was going on when an analyst told her she needed to look at the company's 10-K report really started digging. In the report, she found massive debt, erratic cash flow, and weird transactions. She did the right thing and called Skilling to talk to him before publishing the story. He was rude and called her names because she did not research the company properly.

Then comes Fastow who said that Enron couldn't show earnings details because they had over 1,200 trading books and didn't want just anyone to have access to those books. No one needs to know where we are making money.

In April, Skilling, now the CEO, attacked the Wall Street analyst, Richard Grubman verbally. Grubman told Skilling that Enron had been the only group that would not give them a balance sheet with their earnings statement.

By July 2001, Enron was reporting revenues of $50.1 billion and beating what the analysts had estimated by 3 cents per share. Their profit margin was staying about 2.1%, and its share price was decreased more than 30% since this same quarter in 2000.

Many serious concerns started popping up. They were having logistical problems with a new broadband trading unit, and all the losses they suffered from that Dabhol Power Project in India. They were facing all kinds of criticism for their role in the California electric crisis.

In August, Skilling said he was leaving. He told everyone it was for personal reasons. I don't think so. Before he left, he had sold 450,000 shares of stock in Enron that came to around $33 million. That being said, he still had over a million shares when he left the company.

Ken Lay was trying to smooth things over; he could see the marbles falling from the bag. It looked like things may be starting to unravel. At this point, Lay was only serving as chairman of the board at Enron. He began assuring all the folks watching the market that just because Skilling had left there wouldn't be any problems with the company going forward. No worries, no problems. He told them he would be taking back over as CEO.

The very next day, Skilling came out and told everyone his real reason for leaving was Enron's falling prices in the stock market.

On August 15, Sherron Watkins, who we have not heard from before now, sent a letter, an anonymous letter as a matter of fact to Ken Lay. In this letter, she outlined to him about the accounting practices of Enron. It went on to say that "I am nervous that Enron will fall apart in this mess of accounting humiliations."

August 22nd, Watkins went to Lay with a six-page letter telling him about Enron's accounting fiasco. Lay told Watkins he would get Enron's own law firm to look over the issues. Watkins warned him that would be a conflict of interest.

By the end of August, Enron's stock kept falling, and Ken Lay named Mark Frevert to some position in the chairman's office and Greg Whalley as president and COO of Wholesale Service.

Lay kept trying to explain away the system of accounting, but his efforts met with very little success. When September 9th rolled around, there was one hedge fund manager that said it seemed as the stock of Enron is being traded under a cloud.

September 11, 2001, happened, the Towers went down, thousands of Americans were dead, New York was in shambles, the Pentagon had been hit, the United States was clearly on the verge of war. The stock market plummeted. Everything shifted away from Enron and all its troubles.

About a month later, Enron said it was going to start the process of selling off its lower-margin assets and focus on the core business which was electricity and gas trading. It meant selling Portland Electric, Northwest Natural Gas for about $1.9 billion and looking at possibly selling its 65% share of the Dabhol power plant in India.

October 15th, Enron's law firm made the announcement that Enron had not done anything wrong with its accounting practices because Andersen had been approving each issue.

October 16th, Enron then came out and announced that they had restatements to all its financial statements covering the years 1997 up to 2000 that were necessary for correcting the accounting violations.

The restatements reduced earnings by $613 million! Increased liabilities by the end of 2000 by $628 million, and reduced the equity by the end of 2000 by $1.2 billion.

Enron's team of managers said the losses were due mostly to losses by investment, and money that had to be spent to restructure its broadband unit.

Fastow, told the Enron Board of Directors October 22nd, that he alone made $30 million just from compensation while managing the LJM partnerships. That one day alone, price per share of stock went from $20.65 down by $5.40 after the SEC announced it was going to investigate suspicious deals by Enron.

In their attempts to explain billion-dollar charges and calm down investors, Enron told about "share settled costless collar arrangements," "derivative instruments which eliminated the contingent nature of existing restricted forward contracts," and strategies "to hedge certain merchant investments and other assets."

Two days later, October 25th, Lay fired Fastow. Enron's stock was now at $16.41. It had lost half its worth in just a little over a week.

October 27th, Enron started buying back its commercial paper which came to about $3.3 billion. It was just an effort to calm investor fears that Enron didn't have any cash. To do this, Enron re-purchased this cash by depleting all its credit at many banks. Enron's debt rating was still investment-grade, and its bonds had been trading at slightly less, it was making future sales a problem.

As October was closing, pressing concerns were starting to be raised. Enron executives would only accept questions in a written format.

At the end of October, Enron was having trouble hanging on. And the big credit rating companies were already preparing to slate them for a downgrade. It would force Enron to give out millions of stock shares to cover guaranteed loans, and that would decrease the value of what stock they had left.

October 29th, because of growing concerns that Enron probably did not have sufficient cash, rumors started the rounds that Enron was trying to borrow another $1-2 billion. The very next day, as they feared would happen, Enron's credit rating went down to two levels above what they call 'junk status.'

Enron was on the eve of a full out SEC formal investigation.

To the rescue comes Dynegy, a cross-town rival. The board of Dynegy, that was based in Houston, all voted late at night,

November 7th to buy Enron at a very small price of $8 billion in stocks.

Chevron Texaco, a part of Dynegy, would throw in $2.5 billion cash, it would be $1 billion at first, and then they would give them the rest when the deal was finalized. Dynegy would take on all the $13 billion in Enron debt. The deal was firmed up on November 8th, 2001.

Every day, more bad news just kept spewing forth. November 9th, out came another significant correction about Enron's earnings. It said there was a reduction of $591 million of the stated revenue. Those revisions eliminated almost any profit for 1997 and massive cuts for other years.

Even knowing about this, Dynegy said it was going to buy Enron. The companies were just waiting to get an official assessment about the possible sale from the credit bureau to hopefully understand what effect the completion would have on both of their credit ratings.

Credit issues for Enron were getting more precarious. About that time, they were making the buyout public, Enron's credit rating went down to one notch above junk status. The credit bureau told Enron if they were not bought that their credit score would be dropped to junk status.

It did not help matters when people found out that Ken Lay would get $60 million as a fee for 'change of control' when Dynegy took over. This was while so many Enron staff had seen their life savings ravaged by 90% in just one year. Some of the married couples lost as much as $900,000.

In mid-November, Enron said it was going to sell $8 billion of their underperforming assets and reduce its scale for the mere sake of financial stability. November 19th, they had to tell the public that they owed $9 billion before the end of 2002.

November 21st, Wall Street felt that Dynegy should not proceed with the deal to buy out Enron. Enron showed in a 10-Q filing that all that money they had just borrowed, about $5 billion, was gone in 50 days. Analysts came unglued when they found this out.

The SEC filed civil fraud against Andersen.

November 28th, Dynegy said forget it, we are not going to buy Enron, and Enron's credit rating became junk status. Its stock price was $0.61 by the end of the day. Enron was set up for the "perfect storm."

Enron, it was thought should have had about $23 billion from outstanding debt and guaranteed loans both.

Enron's operations in Europe filed bankruptcy November 3oth and filed Chapter 11. It was the largest bankruptcy in the history of the United States, until the next year when WorldCom beat them out.

The day that Enron filed, all their employees were told, "Pack your stuff up. You have thirty minutes to get out of this building." How horrible that must have been for them. Almost 62% of all 15,000 employees' retirement plans were relying on their Enron stock, and it was GONE!

January 17, 2002, Enron fires Arthur Andersen. It no longer wants it to be its auditing firm and cites that its accounting advice and because they destroyed all the documents is why they were firing their firm. Andersen could not let it go. They countered back with the fact that it ended when Enron filed bankruptcy.

Andersen was always sloppy in their work, but that is what Enron wanted. So, they seemed to deserve each other.

January 13th, 2002 – It Was Not Going to be a Good Year

George W. Bush was approaching his one year anniversary of being inaugurated as President of the United States. The War in Afghanistan was closing down, but he had found himself tied up in the scandal, ENRON scandal.

Enron was now not just under criminal investigation, but double criminal investigation.

Tens of thousands of people/employee's retirement funds and life savings were gone in what had seemed like a blink of an eye. But, not really, that money had gone and lined the pockets of executive directors. It climbed all the way to John Ashcroft, the federal Attorney General. Ashcroft recused himself from the investigation of Enron because he too had been the recipient of money from them.

Vice-President Dick Cheney was not exempt. He was questioned as to his dealings and details of his relationship with Enron.

The public has become aware of the fact that the Bush bunch has been 'beholden' to the energy empire. Even before the Afghan war, there was an 'Energy Task Force' that favored industry that seemed to be Cheney's primary concern, while he came to his office from one of the largest oil equipment companies in the world.

The first day of Ken Lay's trial; he was the chairman and founder of Enron, and now he was being charged with seven counts of conspiracy and fraud.

Mr. Skilling, he is there too. He was Chief Executive, and he was facing dozens of counts, insider trading, conspiracy, and fraud.

Lay and Skilling were the main faces of Enron, but there were others who were there in supporting parts. There are some who admitted to helping to rig the profit increases and hiding the debts and the losses. There were others who tried to be whistleblowers and got nowhere.

Andrew Fastow, the Chief Financial Officer, he avoided the big spotlight. He left that all to Ken Lay and Skilling. He was one of the first ones hired at Enron. He raised large amounts of capital that were needed so Enron could move forward in the natural gas industry and to blaze trails where no one had gone before as a groundbreaking energy powerhouse.

Mr. Fastow entered his guilty plea two years prior, but he worked with others in the company so they could disguise Enron's finances that were deteriorating right before their eyes. He is the one that worked to set up the complex 'off the books' partnerships that were used by Enron, so they did not have to disclose any losses. He used connections, to defraud millions to benefit himself from Enron.

His wife, Lea, she had worked at Enron too, as an assistant treasurer. She got involved in the fraud. She pleads guilty to some misdemeanor tax offense because she did not report some of the gains earned from Andrew Fastow's accounting fraud.

As part of his plea, Andrew Fastow, 44 at the time, faced ten years' imprisonment and decided to cooperate with the federal prosecutors.

There was Ben F. Glisan Jr. who joined Enron in 1996 after he had worked for Arthur Andersen. While working with Andersen, he worked mostly at Enron. He too became part of the "inner circle" and developed and executed many financing schemes to hide Enron's losses.

In 2000, he was appointed as corporate treasurer. Sherron S. Watkins told Congress this was like, "letting the fox in the henhouse."

Mr. Fastow and Mr. Glisan were two among four senior executives of Enron who invested secretly in Southampton Place partnership. Mr. Glisan who spent $5,800, in just a few weeks saw a return close to $1 million. He later gave it all back.

Mr. Glisan was originally indicted on 24 charges of conspiracy, money laundering, and fraud. In 2003, he pleaded guilty to one count of conspiracy to commit securities and wire fraud. At that time, he was serving a 5-year sentence in a federal prison in Texas.

Mr. Glisan's plea put him under no obligation to cooperate with officials, he did testify in 2004 in the prosecution of a criminal case held against four investment bankers from Merrill Lynch and two executives who had worked at Enron.

They had been charged with conspiracy in allowing Enron to fake its profits late in 1999 by a fraudulent sale of Nigerian electrical barges to Merrill. One of the Enron employees and all four of the Merrill execs were convicted. Mr. Glisan was placed on the potential witnesses list for the trials of Skilling and Lay.

Mr. Glisan grew up in Texas, 30 minutes outside of Houston. He was married and had two school-age children at the time.

Lou Lung Pai, which we have not heard of until now, was still a bit player in the scheme of things. He is an interesting fellow anyway. I hate not to mention him, just because of his story.

Mr. Pai (pronounced "pie") was the head of several different divisions while at Enron, he sold contracts that they would provide electricity and natural gas to companies for long periods which was under the Enron Energy Service Division. He had been born in Nanjing, China but emigrated to the U.S. with his parents when he was about two years old. Pai had attended the University of Maryland and earned his Master's in economics. He had worked for the SEC before coming to Enron in 1986.

He was considered to be kind of prickly. He was bad to run up large bills on the company's dime at strip clubs. He had an affair with some exotic dancer that ended his marriage in 1999, and he had to sell most of his Enron stock just to settle his divorce. Mr. Pai's take away from Enron was more than

$271 million. It was the largest of any Enron employee.

Mr. Pai, resigned six months before the filing of bankruptcy, and has been questioned by the investigators but was never charged with any wrongdoing. He said he was never involved in the promotion of selling Enron stock and didn't know anything about off the books accounting. He is on a witness list for the defense for Lay and Skilling.

Mr. Pai did marry his exotic dancer with whom he had the affair; in case you are wondering. They have a daughter and did live in the Houston suburb of Sugar Land, before the trials where they had a stable for training and breeding horses. Mr. Pai did own a 77,500-acre ranch in Colorado, but sold it.

Kenneth Rice, Salesman from the Broadband Unit and who held many posts during his twenty years at Enron. He grew up on his family's farm in Nebraska; got his engineering degree at the University of Nebraska; went on for an MBA at Creighton University in Omaha.

He was a great salesman. He loved to race motorcycles and Ferraris, and Skillings loved him. They went on trips together to Baja, Mexico, the Australian Outback, and Patagonia.

But, he got in trouble too. I hope it was worth it. He was indicted on more than 40, yes, I said 40 charges. They included fraud and conspiracy. He, along with other execs at Enron in the broadband division had been accused of misleading others about the capabilities of what technology they had and their division's performance, therefore resulting in fake inflation of Enron's stock value.

The indictment states that he sold his 1.2 million shares and got more than $76 million. In 2004, he pleaded guilty to ONE count of securities fraud and then agreed to cooperate with the feds. All the other charges were then dropped! The length of his prison term at that time had not been determined. He was also to testify against Ken Lay and Skilling.

Along with his plea, he has agreed to forfeit, cash, cars, a vacation home in Colorado and property that totals $13.7 million. At the time of the trials he was living in Bellaire, outside Houston. He was married to his high school sweetheart, who is a pediatrician and they had four children.

There was Greg Whalley, another good ole boy who was a president at Enron at one time or other. It seemed like everyone at one time, or the other was a president or a CEO of the company. He created pretend futures on contracts for "Popsicles."

When he cornered the market with his other Enron traders, he set it up for an entire truckload of Popsicles that would be delivered to the 'trading floor" as his way of payment for fellow traders. But, the truck had problems on the way there. It broke down, but they still got their Popsicles.

That was only one way that Whalley would loosen up fellow traders and got to be such a popular person in Enron's trading operation.

He was brash, but was so fun-loving, it made him a rising-star. He joined Enron in 1992 right out of Stanford and went straight to the top in Enron.

After Skilling had left, Lay put Whalley in as president of the company. A few weeks in, when Whalley realized what a mess things were in, he fired Fastow without waiting for anyone to say grace over the fact.

Whalley, age 43 at the time, would not return e-mail messages or phone calls to comment on Fastow's termination.

After the collapse of Enron, Whalley was questioned by the feds. He cooperated, but a legal cloud followed him and led to a Swiss bank, to terminate him right after it acquired the trading operations of Enron in 2002.

He then jumped to Centaurus Energy, a Hedge Fund in Houston that had been founded by John Arnold, and he had worked under Whalley at Enron. While at Centaurus, Whalley was put in charge to develop new trade strategies.

Nancy Temple, an attorney for Andersen and had come from a law firm in Chicago. She was a special litigator for issues to do with accounting liability.

Andersen wound up with a $7 million penalty against them because of their shredding of the documents. At the time of the trial, it was the largest fine ever given to an accounting firm. Gee, it just was not good to even know Enron or anyone who worked there.

Andersen's relationship with Enron proved to be the costliest. In early 2002, right after Enron collapsed, Andersen was charged with destroying documents related to all its work where it audited Enron bring on an obstruction of justice charge.

Andersen was told to surrender its C.P.A. License in 2002. It caused 85,000 staff members to lose their jobs. The U.S. Supreme Court later overturned the conviction and allowed Andersen to go ahead and practice as before.

When the jury heard, the criminal case brought against Andersen, they focused on the advice Ms. Temple had given to David Duncan, who was Andersen's head partner for the Enron Account in the fall of 2001. The jurors decided that Ms. Temple had not advised references to the concerns of Andersen's about removing Enron's accounting from the memorandum.

Early in the case, the prosecutors presented an e-mail message that Ms. Temple had sent out to Andersen employees during October, and it was about the firm's "document retention" policy.

The prosecutors felt it had a subtle message in it to destroy all files related to Enron. When Jurors were interviewed afterwards, they said that the shredding had nothing to do with their decisions about anything.

Ms. Temple, in 2002 was married and had an infant son, and she continues in law practice in Chicago.

Rebecca Mark, she was the company's little Global Ambassador. She trotted the globe in her mini-skirt and stiletto heels. It is said she covered the various business development divisions internationally for the company

She came from a small town in Missouri and two different times was on Fortune's index of 50 most powerful business women. She lost favor at Enron because of some bad bets, one of which was a $3 billion bad investment in that power plant in India. It brought on accusations that Enron negotiated a bad deal that was not fair for the 'local' government.

Enron made her resign in August 2000. She sold her shares right after she left and got $82.5 million.

When the trial was going on, Ms. Mark agreed to give back $5.2 million. It was considered her part of a $13 million settlement with shareholders of Enron. A judge did not find any wrongdoing on her part in selling her shares.

At the time, she was Rebecca Mark-Jusbasche. She lived in her three different homes. One in Colorado, one in Mexico and one in Houston. She married a Michael Jusbasche who is a businessman from Bolivia.

Sherron S. Watkins our little Whistle Blower. She will always be remembered as trying to do the right thing.

At the time, she still lived in Southampton in Houston.

She has written a book about the fall of Enron and has a consulting practice which advises other companies on their governance issues. She also lectures around the country.

Vincent Kaminski – he sounded the alarm, but no one would listen to him. He kept warning his supervisors that Fastow was doing some unethical stuff and it was going to catch up with all of them.

In the fall of 2001, Kaminski's disgust got the best of him, and his anger was getting worse. He started refusing to sign documents that related to anything to do with Raptors that Fastow had made up. He told his team of internal consultants to not do any work for Enron's finance department.

In March 2001, he went in to Mr. Glisan, Enron's treasurer. He showed him a report that proved Fastow's deals had put them in imminent danger for Enron to survive.

Mainly due to stock price "triggers" which would be how their bank loans would be repaid in the event Enron's credit rating would be downgraded and their stock prices would fall.

Kaminski, was from Poland, educated as an economist, earned a business degree, was with Enron until 2002.

In about 2003, Mr. Kaminski was 57, landed at Citigroup. He is well known in the energy world because of his loyalty to all the brainy minds he would recruit from worldwide top universities. While Enron collapsed, he helped all 50 of his prior research members find jobs.

The Two Dirtiest Dogs In The Fight ...

And so, they were, the two dirtiest dogs in this fight and they were being brought in for the justice that was waiting on them.

Ken Lay and Jeff Skillings were both found Guilty of fraud and conspiracy of one of the biggest if not the biggest of corporate fraud cases in America.

There was a jury of four men and eight women who listened to four months of testimony and deliberated for six days before making their decisions.

Skillings was found guilty of insider trading, false statements, fraud and 19 counts of conspiracy. Honestly, I do not know how they could separate it all out; it was such a confusion web of lies and distortion. His expected release from prison will be February 21, 2019. He is currently still serving time in Montgomery, Alabama.

He was fined $45 million.

Lay they found he was guilty of fraud and six counts of conspiracy. In a separately held bench trial, a judge also found him to be guilty of false statements and four counts of fraud.

Lay early on participated in defrauding. He knew about Enron's quickly deteriorating performance in its business unit, and he made one after the other false and public statements about how good Enron's financial condition was doing. He was the CEO and was reviewing the public filings, press releases, and taking part in conference calls with analysts over investments.

Lay knew that all the credit rating agencies had no idea about how bad Enron's prepay obligations were and they had no way of knowing as it was not published in Enron's public filings.

After Skillings had left, Lay knew the real reason. Skillings had told him that there was nothing that could be done to stop Enron's stock from dropping. Lay approved a press release saying Skillings was leaving for personal reasons when Lay knew better.

Later that same day, Lay had a conference call with worried investment analysts. Lay kept telling them, "there are absolutely no problems that had anything to do with Jeff's departure, there are no accounting issues, no

trading issues, no reserve issues….
unknown, previously unknown problems, issues…I can honestly say that the company is probably in the strongest and best shape…that it's probably ever been in. We've been doubling revenue and doubling income quarter on quarter, year on year for now about the last three years. We expect that to continue to grow very, very strong…."

Senior management kept telling Ken how bad things were. How it was deteriorating right before their eyes.

Lay kept up the farce. In August and September of 2001, he was still telling his employees that there were no accounting problems, there were no issues with reserves, and they did not have to worry about any more shoes falling at Enron. He told them the third quarter was looking just great. Our balance sheet is strong, and we got great numbers. He even told them that in the last couple of months that he had bought more shares.

Third quarter earnings were a bust. Lay made up some crazy excuse to analysts that the reason for the shareholder equity being reduced by $1.2 billion was because they were terminating the Raptor program early. When, in reality it was because of a huge accounting error.

October and November 2001 Lay just kept digging his grave a little deeper, well, really deep if you ask me. Deeper than the required 6-8 foot. He kept telling everyone that Enron was not trying to cover anything up.

He told the auditors that they had looked over the books with a fine-tooth comb and there are no additional problems that should be forthcoming. But, he knew that its international dealings and assets were being assessed in the billions above their fair market value.

Lay continued to tell the employees that their liquidity was great. All the time he was telling this he knew that he had to put up his beloved pipelines for collateral to get $1 billion in a bank loan and his only source left for liquidity was $3 billion in credit. Lay also did not share that he had ever so quietly sold off $65 million in Enron stock during 2001.

He also took money from his line of credit that totaled $7.5 million at the time Enron was falling apart.

Lay, after he was convicted, was outside of the courthouse and made this statement: "We believe that God, in fact, is in control, and indeed He does work all things for good for those who love the Lord."

Ken Lay never lived to be sentenced. He died July 5, 2006 in Colorado while on vacation of a heart attack in the early morning hours.

When the jurors were speaking to the reporters after the verdicts had been read, they stated it was one of the hardest if not the hardest decision they had ever had to make.

But, they did agree that all the evidence and all the witnesses that the prosecution brought before them was just too strong to ignore.

It seemed none of the jurors cared for Fastow. They all realized that Fastow had been guilty, and his treachery was what got him in trouble and the reason he was there was because he had cut a deal with the prosecutors, so to keep up with his end of the bargain, he had to testify against Lay and Skilling so he would get a lighter sentence.

One juror, Wendy Vaughn, who owned two businesses in Houston stated that when the trial started, she had admired both Skilling and Lay's intelligence and their talent as businessmen. But it was so sad to see what they did with it in the end.

As their convictions were being read in court; it is said that Skilling was standing stone-faced. His wife and children were NOT there.

When Lay's time came for his verdict to be read, his own daughter, Elizabeth Lay Vittore, who also served as one of his attorneys on his case, started sobbing.

Lay's wife, Linda kept clutching his hand and wiped her tears away quietly. The rest of his children were on the front row with other family members. One son put his hands to his face and wept.

Lay held his wife's hand and just looked straight ahead. He still expressed shock with the verdict and kept maintaining his innocence. He said that no matter what has happened here I am a very blessed man.

Skilling when he got out of the courtroom said, "We fought the good fight. Some things work. Some things don't." "Obviously, I am disappointed, but that's how the system works."

Enron employees rejoiced at the verdicts.

Those Who Suffered – It Was Not Right

There were nice people like Pat Betteridge, who worked at Portland Electric in Oregon, who remembered the claims Ken Lay came by and made to him. He told him that Enron liked to think of themselves as the Microsoft of the energy part of the world.

Poor Betteridge had taken his $300,000 he had put back for retirement and bought 3,500 shares, and when all was said and done, he was penniless and too old to start over.

Pat said if he did electrical work as bad as the Enron Execs had done theirs he would either be doing time or have his license yanked.

The shareholders of Enron lost over $74 billion in four years BEFORE the bankruptcy and ($40-$45 billion of it was because of fraud).

Enron had almost $67 billion it still owed people. It owed shareholders, employees, and creditors and none of them got anything aside from severance pay from Enron. To try and pay the creditors, Enron had auctions to sell pipelines, logo signs, photographs, and art.

May 2004, 20,000 of Enron's prior employees finally won a suit of $85 million of $2 billion they lost from their pensions. Each of the employees wound up with $3,100.

In 2005, the investors got another settlement that came from several banks for $4.2 billion.

In 2008, there was a $7.2 billion settle for a $40-billion lawsuit that was finally reached for the shareholders. It was given to the University of California, 1.5 million groups and individuals.

The law firm that represented all this mess received $688 million in their fees.

Because of this terrible fiasco, the Sarbanes-Oxley Act was born. The act itself almost matches all the things that went terribly wrong with Enron point by point and how it was to be prevented.

The Securities and Exchange Commission also made some changes to the NYSE:

- All companies must have a majority of independent directors

- Independent directors must comply with an elaborate definition of independent directors.
- The compensation committee, nominating committee, and audit committee shall consist of independent directors.
- All audit committee members should be financially literate. In addition, at least one member of the audit committee is required to have accounting or related financial management expertise.
- In addition to its regular sessions, the board should hold additional sessions without management.

The sickening part was the big wheels at Enron were taking advantage of knowing when to get out and selling off their stock and making a run for it, while everyone else was left holding an empty bag. Jail time is not enough for something like that.

So, was there any good that came from all of this? Maybe, I guess, who knows? For those who do follow the law and have some moral standards and ethics about them, I would say yes. For others, it will not make a bit of difference.

July 26, 2002, saw the Fraud Bill be 'rushed' through Congress. Its main aim was to have more supervision and to punish those companies that were not following the law.

Its aim, of course, to reassure investors that corporate America could be trusted.

Maximum jail sentences were going to be increased up to 20 years for mail and wire fraud. A new crime that when committed on securities fraud will have a 25-year maximum stint in jail.

Was this bill for real? Or was it just a political gesture?

Conclusion

Enron epitomized corruption that seems to be in every thread in corporate America and gives us a glimpse of all the anti-social methods that are used by our financial 'elitist' so they may accrue vast amounts of personal wealth during stock market booms and at the expense of the little man. It further shines a light on the remedies needed for the "magic of the market" and deregulation.

As I reflect on the key individuals involved; I do not understand how they could have slept at night. I say this as Ken Lay's upbringing does not differ that much from mine. But, then, I have never been a person to live lavishly, I live life being happy, trying to live in the moment.

It seems, and this is only my opinion, that Ken Lay lived in a constant state of denial. He could not bear to see the empire he had built fail. He had such pipe dreams for Enron. It made him someone. The someone, his father, had never become.

In his early years, he had worked hard to get where he had gotten, but things got so much easier for him that when the cards started to fall, he was in such denial that he just could not accept the fact that it was over.

I am not sure he ever did. I believe in his mind that everything would have worked out if everyone would have just kept going. It was like he had almost come to the point of a mental breakdown.

My heart goes out to the employees of Enron. It forever changed their lives, and I am sure they will never be able to trust anyone with their money again. I do not blame them.

So, you have read the book, you have heard the stories, what do you think?

CPSIA information can be obtained
at www.ICGtesting.com
Printed in the USA
BVHW042306200223
658901BV00001B/7